Building Large Language Model(LLM Apps)

What Are LLM Apps?

Large Language Model (LLM) Apps are software applications that leverage the power of large- scale language models to understand, generate, and interact with human language. These applications utilize advanced natural language processing (NLP) techniques to perform a variety of tasks, such as text generation, translation, summarization, question answering, and sentiment analysis. The core of these apps is a pre-trained language model that has been fine-tuned for specific tasks or domains, enabling the application to provide intelligent, context-aware responses and perform complex language-related functions.

The Importance of LLMs in Modern Applications The integration of LLMs into modern applications has revolutionized the way we interact with technology. Here are a few reasons why LLMs are crucial:

1. **Enhanced User Experience:** LLMs provide more natural and intuitive interactions, making technology more accessible and easier to use.

2. **Automation and Efficiency:** LLMs can automate complex language tasks, reducing the need for human intervention and increasing efficiency.

3. **Scalability:** LLM-powered applications can handle large volumes of data and interactions, making them suitable for use in various industries, from customer service to healthcare.

4. **Innovation:** The capabilities of LLMs drive innovation, leading to the development of

new products and services that were

previously unimaginable.

Understanding Large Language Models

History and Evolution of LLMs

The development of large language models is a significant

milestone in the field of artificial intelligence (AI) and NLP. The

journey began with simple statistical models that relied on

hand- crafted features and evolved into complex neural

network-based models. Here's a brief overview of this evolution:

1. **Early NLP Approaches:** Initially, NLP tasks were handled using rule-based systems and simple machine learning algorithms. These methods required extensive manual effort to define rules and features.

2. **Introduction of Neural Networks:** The advent of neural networks marked a turning point, allowing models to learn features directly from data. Recurrent Neural Networks (RNNs) and Long Short-Term Memory networks (LSTMs) became popular for sequential data.

3. **Rise of Transformers:** The introduction of the Transformer architecture in 2017

revolutionized the field. Transformers utilize

self-attention mechanisms, allowing them to process text in

parallel and capture long-range dependencies more

effectively.

4. **Pre-trained Language Models:** Models like

BERT (Bidirectional Encoder Representations from

Transformers) and GPT (Generative Pre- trained

Transformer) demonstrated the power of pre-training on

large text corpora, followed by fine-tuning on specific tasks.

This approach significantly improved performance across

various NLP tasks.

Key Concepts and Terminology

To effectively work with LLMs, it is essential to understand some key concepts and terminology:

- **Tokenization:** The process of converting text into smaller units, such as words or subwords, that can be processed by the model.

- **Embedding:** A representation of words or tokens as dense vectors in a continuous space, capturing their semantic meaning.

- **Attention Mechanism:** A component of the Transformer model that allows it to focus on relevant parts of the input text, improving its ability to capture context.

- **Fine-Tuning:** The process of adapting a pre-trained model to a specific task by training it on a smaller, task-specific dataset.

- **Transfer Learning:** Using knowledge gained from one task to improve performance on another related task, often involving pre- trained models.

Popular LLM Architectures (GPT, BERT, etc.) Several LLM architectures have become popular due to their effectiveness in various NLP tasks:

1.GPT (Generative Pre-trained Transformer):

Developed by OpenAI, GPT is an autoregressive model that generates text by predicting the next token in a sequence. GPT-3, the latest version, is renowned for its impressive text generation capabilities and versatility.

2.BERT (Bidirectional Encoder Representations from Transformers): Created by Google, BERT

is a bidirectional model that considers the context from both directions (left and right) of a token. This makes it highly effective for tasks like question answering and sentiment analysis.

3.T5 (Text-to-Text Transfer Transformer):

Developed by Google, T5 treats all NLP tasks

as a text-to-text problem, making it a highly

flexible model capable of performing various tasks,

including translation and summarization.

4.**XLNet:** An extension of BERT, XLNet improves

on the pre-training process by leveraging a permutation-

based training method, enhancing its ability to capture

dependencies in text.

These architectures have set new benchmarks in NLP and are

the foundation of many cutting-edge applications today.

Understanding their

underlying principles and strengths is crucial for

building effective LLM-powered applications.

Setting Up Your Development Environment

Creating a suitable development environment is a crucial step in building applications with large language models (LLMs). This chapter will guide you through the hardware and software requirements, installing the necessary tools and libraries, and utilizing cloud services for efficient development and deployment.

Hardware and Software Requirements

Hardware Requirements

1.Computing Power:

- **GPU (Graphics Processing Unit):** LLMs, especially during training and fine-tuning, require significant computational power. A GPU accelerates the processing, making it almost indispensable for serious development. NVIDIA GPUs are widely used due to their compatibility with popular deep learning frameworks.

- **RAM:** A minimum of 16GB of RAM is recommended for working with LLMs. For larger models and more extensive datasets, 32GB or more is preferable.

- **Storage:** SSDs (Solid State Drives) are preferred over traditional HDDs (Hard Disk Drives) due to their faster read/write speeds. You'll need ample storage (at least 500GB) to handle large datasets and model checkpoints.

2.Peripheral Requirements:

- **High-Resolution Display:** A high-resolution monitor can enhance productivity by providing more screen real estate for code, documentation, and debugging information.

- **Ergonomic Accessories:** Ergonomic keyboards, mice, and chairs can make long development sessions more comfortable and prevent strain injuries.

Software Requirements

1.Operating System:

- Linux (Ubuntu is highly recommended) is the preferred OS for machine learning and deep learning tasks due to its compatibility with various tools and libraries. However, Windows and macOS can also be used with proper

configuration.

2.Programming Languages:

- **Python:** The primary language for

  developing with LLMs due to its extensive libraries

  and community support. Ensure you have Python 3.6

  or later installed.

3.Integrated Development Environment (IDE):

- Popular IDEs include VS Code, PyCharm, and

  Jupyter Notebook. These tools offer useful features

  like syntax highlighting, code completion, and

  debugging.

Installing Necessary Tools and Libraries

1.Package Management:

- **Anaconda:** A distribution that simplifies package management and deployment. It comes with Conda, a package, dependency, and environment manager.

- **pip:** The package installer for Python. It's crucial for installing Python packages that aren't available through Conda.

2.Deep Learning Frameworks:

- **TensorFlow:** Install TensorFlow via pip (**pip install tensorflow**) or Conda (**conda install tensorflow**).

- **PyTorch:** Install PyTorch via pip (**pip install torch**) or Conda (**conda install pytorch**).

3.NLP Libraries:

- **Hugging Face Transformers:** Install via pip (**pip install transformers**). This library provides a straightforward interface for working with LLMs like GPT, BERT, etc.

- **spaCy:** Useful for traditional NLP tasks. Install via pip (**pip install spacy**).

4.Other Essential Libraries:

- **NumPy:** For numerical operations (**pip install numpy**).

- **Pandas:** For data manipulation (**pip install pandas**).

- **scikit-learn:** For machine learning tasks (**pip install scikit-learn**).

- **Matplotlib/Seaborn:** For data visualization (**pip install matplotlib seaborn**).

Working with Cloud Services

Given the resource-intensive nature of LLMs, leveraging cloud services can be highly beneficial. Cloud platforms provide scalable infrastructure, which is particularly useful for training large models and handling big datasets.

1.**Popular Cloud Providers:**

- **AWS (Amazon Web Services):** Offers powerful instances with GPUs, such as the EC2 P3 and G4 instances.

- **Google Cloud Platform (GCP):** Provides Tensor Processing Units (TPUs) and GPU instances. AI Platform simplifies the

deployment of machine learning models.

- **Microsoft Azure:** Offers a range of GPU

  instances and Azure Machine Learning services.

2.Setting Up Cloud Instances:

- **Choosing the Right Instance:** Select

  instances with GPUs for deep learning tasks. AWS EC2,

  GCP Compute Engine, and Azure VMs offer various GPU

  options.

- **Configuration:** Install necessary libraries

  and frameworks on your cloud instance.

You can use Docker to create a containerized environment, ensuring consistency across different setups.

3. Storage Solutions:

- **AWS S3, GCP Cloud Storage, Azure Blob Storage:** These services offer scalable storage solutions for datasets and model checkpoints.

- **Mounting Cloud Storage:** You can mount cloud storage buckets to your instances for seamless data access and management.

4.Cost Management:

- **Spot Instances/Preemptible VMs:** These
  options can significantly reduce costs but come with the
  risk of instance termination when demand is high.

- **Monitoring and Budgeting Tools:** Use
  tools provided by cloud platforms to monitor usage
  and set budgets to avoid unexpected expenses.

By setting up a robust development environment with the right
hardware, software, and cloud infrastructure, you'll be well-
equipped to build

and deploy applications powered by large

language models. This foundational setup is critical to ensuring

that your development process is efficient, scalable, and capable

of handling the complexities associated with LLMs.

Data Preparation

Gathering and Cleaning Data

Gathering Data

1.Sources of Data:

- **Public Datasets:** Utilize publicly available datasets from sources like Kaggle, UCI Machine Learning Repository, and academic publications.

- **Web Scraping:** Collect data from websites using tools like BeautifulSoup, Scrapy, or Selenium. Ensure you comply with legal and ethical guidelines.

- **APIs:** Access structured data through APIs provided by services like Twitter, Reddit, or public data APIs.

2.Types of Data:

- **Text Data:** Articles, books, social media posts, and transcriptions.

- **Structured Data:** Tables and spreadsheets with labeled information.

- **Unstructured Data:** Raw text that needs to be processed and structured.

Cleaning Data

1.Handling Missing Data:

- **Remove Missing Values:** If the amount of missing data is small, remove those entries.

- **Impute Missing Values:** Replace missing values with a placeholder or estimated value.

2. **Removing Noise:**

- **Stop Words:** Remove common words (like "and", "the") that do not contribute much meaning.

- **Special Characters:** Remove unnecessary punctuation, special characters, and digits.

- **Normalization:** Convert text to lowercase and perform stemming or lemmatization to reduce words to their base forms.

3.Tokenization:

- **Word Tokenization:** Split text into individual words or tokens.

- **Sentence Tokenization:** Split text into sentences.

1.Manual Annotation:

- **Human Annotators:** Employ experts or crowdsource tasks through platforms like Amazon Mechanical Turk to manually label data.

- **Annotation Tools:** Use tools like Labelbox, Prodigy, or doccano to facilitate the annotation process.

2.Automated Annotation:

- **Rule-Based Systems:** Use predefined rules to automatically label data.

- **Pre-trained Models:** Utilize pre-trained models to generate labels, followed by human verification.

3.Annotation Guidelines:

- **Clear Instructions:** Provide annotators with clear guidelines and examples.

- **Consistency Checks:** Implement inter-annotator agreement measures to ensure consistency.

Handling Imbalanced Data

1.Understanding Imbalance:

- **Distribution Analysis:** Visualize class distributions using bar plots or pie charts to identify imbalance.

- **Metrics Impact:** Recognize how imbalance affects metrics like accuracy, precision, recall, and F1-score.

2.Techniques to Handle Imbalance:

- **Resampling:**

  - **Oversampling:** Increase the number of instances in the minority class using techniques like SMOTE (Synthetic Minority Over-sampling Technique).

- **Undersampling:** Reduce the number of instances in the majority class.

Class Weights:

- **Weighted Loss Function:** Adjust the loss function to penalize misclassifications of the minority class more heavily.

Data Augmentation:

- **Text Augmentation:** Generate synthetic data by paraphrasing, translating, or using generative models.

Training Large Language Models

Training Basics and Best Practices

1.Model Selection:

- Choose a model architecture that suits your task (e.g., GPT for text generation, BERT for classification).

2.Training Process:

- **Initialization:** Start with pre-trained weights if available.

- **Batch Size:** Choose an appropriate batch size that fits your GPU memory.

- **Learning Rate:** Use a learning rate scheduler to adjust the learning rate during training.

3.Best Practices:

- **Regular Monitoring:** Monitor loss and performance metrics regularly.

- **Early Stopping:** Implement early stopping to prevent overfitting.

- **Checkpointing:** Save model checkpoints periodically to avoid losing progress.

1.Data Parallelism:

- **Split Batches:** Distribute different batches of data across multiple GPUs or machines.

2.Model Parallelism:

- **Split Model:** Distribute different parts of the model across multiple GPUs or machines.

3.Frameworks and Tools:

- **Horovod:** A distributed training framework for TensorFlow, Keras, and PyTorch.

- **Distributed TensorFlow/PyTorch:** Use built-in functionalities for distributed training.

1.Monitoring Tools:

- **TensorBoard:** Visualize metrics, model graphs, and histograms.

- **Weights & Biases:** Track experiments, visualize metrics, and collaborate with team members.

2.Debugging Techniques:

- **Gradient Inspection:** Check for exploding or vanishing gradients.

- **Loss Trends:** Analyze loss curves to identify issues like overfitting or underfitting.

- **Profiling:** Use profilers to identify bottlenecks in the training process.

Fine-Tuning Pre-trained Models

Understanding Fine-Tuning

Fine-tuning involves taking a pre-trained model and further training it on a specific task with a smaller, task-specific dataset. This approach leverages the general language understanding of the pre-trained model and adapts it to the specific nuances of the new task.

Techniques for Effective Fine-Tuning

1.Layer Freezing:

- Freeze the initial layers of the model and only train the later layers to preserve the pre-trained knowledge.

2.Learning Rate Adjustment:

- Use a lower learning rate for fine-tuning compared to training from scratch to avoid overwriting the pre-trained weights.

3.Gradual Unfreezing:

- Gradually unfreeze layers and fine-tune them one at a time to stabilize training.

4.Task-Specific Tokens:

- Introduce special tokens or embeddings

  relevant to the specific task to improve performance.

Case Studies and Examples

1.Sentiment Analysis:

- Fine-tune a pre-trained BERT model on a sentiment

  analysis dataset (e.g., movie reviews) to classify text

  as positive or negative.

2.Named Entity Recognition (NER):

- Fine-tune a pre-trained BERT model on an NER dataset to identify entities like names, dates, and locations in text.

3.Question Answering:

- Fine-tune a pre-trained model like RoBERTa on a question-answering dataset (e.g., SQuAD) to answer questions based on a given context.

4.Text Generation:

- Fine-tune a GPT model on a dataset of creative writing to generate text in a specific style or genre.

By following these guidelines and best practices,

you'll be well-equipped to prepare your data, train large

language models effectively, and fine- tune pre-trained models

to suit your specific needs. This comprehensive approach

ensures robust, high-performing models tailored to your

application's requirements.

Developing LLM Applications

Designing User Interfaces for LLM Apps

User Experience (UX) Design:

1.Intuitive Design:

- Ensure the interface is intuitive and easy to

    navigate. Use clear labels, concise instructions, and

    a logical flow of information.

2.Feedback Mechanisms:

- Provide users with immediate feedback to their

    inputs. This could be through visual

cues, confirmations, or suggestions to

guide the user.

User Interface (UI) Elements:

1.Text Input Fields:

- Design input fields that allow users to enter text

  easily. Implement features like auto-completion and

  spell check.

2.Response Display:

- Present model responses clearly and concisely. Use

  formatting to highlight key information.

3.Interactive Components:

- Incorporate buttons, sliders, and dropdown menus to allow users to customize their interactions with the model.

Accessibility:

1.Inclusive Design:

- Ensure the app is accessible to users with disabilities. Use screen readers, keyboard navigation, and adjustable text sizes.

2.Multilingual Support:

- Provide support for multiple languages to cater to a diverse user base.

APIs and Frameworks:

1.RESTful APIs:

- Use REST APIs to integrate LLM functionalities into existing systems. Ensure APIs are well-documented and provide necessary endpoints for various tasks.

2.GraphQL:

- Utilize GraphQL for more flexible queries and interactions with LLMs.

Middleware:

1.Message Brokers:

- Use message brokers like RabbitMQ or Kafka to handle communication between different components of your system.

2.Microservices:

- Implement LLM functionalities as microservices to enable scalability and easier maintenance.

Data Integration:

1.Database Connectivity:

- Ensure seamless integration with your databases for storing and retrieving data.

Use ORM (Object-Relational Mapping)

tools for ease of use.

2.Data Pipelines:

- Establish data pipelines to preprocess data before

  feeding it into LLMs and post- process model outputs.

Building Interactive LLM Features

Conversational Agents:

1.Chatbots:

- Develop chatbots that can handle user queries,

  provide information, and perform

tasks through natural language
conversations.

2.Virtual Assistants:

- Create virtual assistants that can manage schedules,

  send reminders, and perform a variety of user-defined

  tasks.

Content Generation:

1.Text Generation:

- Use LLMs to generate creative content such as

  articles, stories, and social media posts.

2.Summarization:

- Implement summarization features to condense long texts into shorter, more digestible summaries.

Interactive Applications:

1.Language Translation:

- Build applications that translate text from one language to another using LLMs.

2.Sentiment Analysis:

- Develop tools to analyze the sentiment of texts, providing insights into user opinions and feedback.

Natural Language Processing Tasks

Text Generation

1.Creative Writing:

- Use LLMs to generate poems, stories, and articles. Fine-tune models on specific genres to enhance creativity and coherence.

2.Automated Reports:

- Generate business reports, summaries, and insights from data.

Sentiment Analysis

1.Customer Feedback:

- Analyze customer reviews and feedback to gauge sentiment and identify areas for improvement.

2.Social Media Monitoring:

- Monitor social media platforms to track public sentiment on various topics and trends.

Named Entity Recognition

1.Information Extraction:

- Extract names, dates, locations, and other entities from text to build structured data from unstructured sources.

2.Document Annotation:

- Automate the annotation of documents for easier

  data management and retrieval.

Machine Translation

1.Language Services:

- Provide translation services for websites,

  documents, and communication platforms.

2.Localization:

- Localize software and content for different regions and

  languages.

Advanced LLM Techniques

Prompt Engineering

1.Crafting Effective Prompts:

- Design prompts that guide LLMs to produce desired
  outputs. Experiment with different phrasings and
  structures.

2.Context Management:

- Provide sufficient context in prompts to improve
  the relevance and accuracy of responses.

Transfer Learning

1.Domain Adaptation:

- Fine-tune pre-trained models on domain-specific data to improve performance on specialized tasks.

2.Cross-Lingual Training:

- Use transfer learning to train models across multiple languages, enhancing their multilingual capabilities.

Multi-Task Learning

1.Unified Models:

- Train models on multiple tasks simultaneously, improving efficiency and generalization.

2. Task-Specific Layers:

- Add task-specific layers to a shared base model to handle different tasks with a single architecture.

Zero-Shot and Few-Shot Learning

1. Zero-Shot Learning:

- Use models to perform tasks without any task-specific training data. Leverage pre- trained knowledge to generalize across tasks.

2. Few-Shot Learning:

- Train models with a very small amount of task-specific data, demonstrating the ability to quickly adapt to new tasks.

Deployment and Scalability

Deployment Strategies

1.Containerization:

- Use Docker to containerize your applications, ensuring consistent environments across development, testing, and production.

2.Serverless Computing:

- Deploy applications using serverless architectures (e.g., AWS Lambda) to automatically scale based on demand.

Ensuring Scalability and Performance

1.Load Balancing:

- Distribute incoming traffic across multiple instances to

  prevent overloading any single server.

2.Caching:

- Implement caching strategies to reduce latency

  and improve response times for frequently

  accessed data.

Managing Costs

1.Resource Optimization:

- Optimize the use of computational resources by using efficient algorithms and batch processing.

2.Cost Monitoring:

- Use tools to monitor and manage cloud service costs, setting budgets and alerts to avoid unexpected expenses.

Security and Ethics in LLM Apps

Addressing Bias and Fairness

1.Bias Detection:

- Use bias detection tools to identify and mitigate biases in your models.

2.Fairness Audits:

- Conduct regular fairness audits to ensure your applications do not discriminate against any group.

Ensuring Privacy and Security

1.Data Encryption:

- Encrypt data at rest and in transit to protect sensitive information.

2.Access Control:

- Implement strict access control measures to limit who can access and modify data.

Ethical Considerations

1.Transparency:

- Be transparent about how your models work and the data they use.

2.Accountability:

- Establish accountability frameworks to address any issues that arise from the use of your applications.

Case Studies and Real-World Applications

LLMs in Customer Service

1.Automated Support:

- Use chatbots to handle common customer queries, freeing up human agents for more complex issues.

2.Feedback Analysis:

- Analyze customer feedback to identify trends and areas for improvement.

LLMs in Healthcare

1.Medical Record Analysis:

- Use LLMs to extract insights from patient records, improving diagnosis and treatment plans.

2.Patient Interaction:

- Implement virtual assistants to provide patients with information and support.

LLMs in Finance

1.Fraud Detection:

- Analyze transaction data to detect fraudulent activities.

2.Financial Advising:

- Use LLMs to provide personalized financial advice to customers.

Troubleshooting and Optimization

Common Issues and Solutions

1.Overfitting:

- Use regularization techniques and cross-validation to prevent overfitting.

2.Data Quality:

- Ensure high-quality data by cleaning and preprocessing it thoroughly.

Performance Optimization Techniques

1.Model Pruning:

- Reduce model size by pruning unnecessary parameters, improving inference speed.

2.Quantization:

- Convert models to lower precision formats to increase efficiency without significantly impacting performance.

Future Trends and Developments

1.Advancements in LLMs:

- Stay updated with the latest advancements in LLM research and development.

2.Ethical AI:

- Follow the evolving standards and practices in ethical AI development to ensure responsible usage.

By following these guidelines, you can effectively develop, deploy, and maintain applications powered by large language models, ensuring they

are robust, scalable, and ethically sound.

www.ingramcontent.com/pod-product-compliance
Lightning Source LLC
LaVergne TN
LVHW051611050326
832903LV00033B/4452